Machine Learning

An Introduction To Supervised & Unsupervised Learning Algorithms

MICHAEL COLINS

CONTENTS

INTRODUCTION

Welcome to the journey of Machine Learning! The purpose of this book is to introduce machine learning and its algorithms to anyone brave enough to explore this seemingly complex subject. There are a number of books on machine learning published now, but very few of them discuss how algorithms are created. In this book, you will be introduced to a variety of scenarios to give you a better idea of how machine learning algorithms are used today. This book is light on coding, but you will get an overview of how machine learning works and the programming space around it.

Basically, machine learning is making sense of data. If you are familiar with programming concepts like recursion and data structures—like trees—you will be able to grasp the contents of this book much easier. However, if you only have a foggy sense of data and how data structures are organized, you'll still be able to take a thing or two away from this book with a few diligent passes.

We will start off by exploring the subject of classification, which is the process for item labeling. You'll then learn more about logistic regression, which eventually leads to optimization algorithms. Then we'll talk about probability distributions, the Naïve Bayes algorithm, and how those concepts apply to machine learning. We'll delve into decision trees and mull over the use of K-means clustering as well. If you're not sure what all this technical jargon is, that's alright—you'll get an overview of how all these topics apply to machine learning, which will ultimately enable you to have deeper discussions with others in the field.

Technical mechanics aside, we're all very curious about how machine learning will affect careers and future employment in the coming decade, so naturally we'll discuss a few theories in the final chapters. Hopefully by the end of this book, you will have had enough of the right details to shed light for you on the topic of Machine Learning (ML) to get you excited about the possible applications for this up and coming technology. Enjoy!

CHAPTER 1
CLASSIFICATION

Basics of Machine Learning

Jane was having lunch with some friends when she was asked to share about what she's currently working on at work. She answered, "Machine learning." Her friends just looked at her in shock and they were like, "Guys, what is machine learning?" One friend answered, "Cyberdyne Systems T-800." Has anyone of you seen the movie Terminator? It narrates a story of a robot that went against its programming intelligence. Some of Jane's friend were already put off. This book is not going to try to get into conversations about computer programs or the consciousness of artificial intelligence in the current world. When we get to machine learning, a whole new world comes to life because of how the concept of datasets in machines, brings insight into data. This is our definition of learning, not the creation of sentient beings nor cyborg rote memorization.

Machine learning is currently in use, perhaps in places that you would least expect. Let's look at how a normal day looks like when you are interacting with machine learning without you realizing it. Maybe it's one of your friend's graduation ceremony and you are planning to buy a gift, and you have no clue on the gift that you will buy. You go to the internet and search for the perfect gift and several relevant links are displayed. When you search for a card in the search engine, there are about ten relevant links that pop up. When you click any link, it will be factored in the search engine which will begin a process of relating what you are looking for. Next, when you check your emails, the spam folder will be stocked with some crazy adverts about offers of products that you might be interested in.

Next, when you head to the mall to purchase the gift, you buy some towels for your household since you need to replace the old ones. When you get to the cashier to pay for the items, you are awarded a coupon of $2 for a pack of soap. The coupon was created by the register at the cashier's desk, for anyone who was going to purchase a towel. Looking at another instance, when you decide to get a loan from a bank, the process is normally easy; bankers usually access your financial information from their computer database and decide whether to give you a loan, or not.

In all the scenarios we have looked at, there was the presence of machine learning. Companies are using machine learning to improve and change the way business processes are done in all relevant fields of production. Technology is growing at a speed most of us are not able to keep up with. This is making companies evolve and create new business opportunities that are more information driven for both the past and future data.

Are you prepared for machine learning? You are going to find out what machine learning is, where it is being used in your normal daily activities, and how it might be of assistance to you shortly. Lastly, we will talk about common approaches on how to solve problems using machine learning.

What is Machine Learning?

You cannot make anything out of numbers when you have tons of data to look at, it will just be a blur. Machine learning is about making sense of data that you have been given. It embodies heavily on science and mathematics, not to forget other disciplines that come into play on occasion. There are so many possible applications of this solution to change how we live on a daily basis. Every field survives on data, and how to use the data to progress the development of solutions. It is, therefore, safe to say that machine learning is paramount in every field.

Statistics are the essentials of machine learning. To many people, statistics is esoteric to companies that want to lie about to customers about how great their products are. There is even a book on how to for this using statistics. So, one might ask, why are statistics that important? The discipline of engineering is how to apply science to problem-solving. We are used to solving deterministic problems in engineering where our solution always counter our problems all the time.

In this world, we have problems that we do not even understand in full depth. In the 1900's, we were analyzing data with very large computers that were not capable of handling so much data. As time progressed, we have come up with advanced technologies, but at the same time, we have quadrupled the size of data. We can't process all the data in any given field to understand upcoming or overgrown problems, with all this data that keep popping every minute of the day. For instance, it is difficult to model the motivation of humans.

In the social sciences field, having 60% accuracy is considered as a successful measure all the time. We have not even managed to get to that limit, let alone breaking that ceiling.

1. Data deluge and the application of sensors

Over the last decade, we have created more data than the world has ever created since the beginning of time. This is all thanks to the world wide web, but of late, there has been a rising number of nonhuman data sources coming online. The technology that runs behind the sensors has been in existence, but what is new is connecting them to the world wide web. Let us look at the following examples to learn about data.

A) In 1989, a deadly earthquake struck in the North of California, and it killed hundreds and injured thousands. Similarly, an earthquake struck Haiti and killed over 200,000 people in 2010. After the earthquakes occur, scientist analyzed the data from the earthquakes and they were able to predict the next earthquakes.

B) some studies showed that there was a flaw in the original study on the earthquakes. The thing is, it is very costly to redo such a study because you have to factor in, how the study will be done, the equipment needed, the land that will be used for the study. It's very hectic planning for such a study. Alternatively, instead of burdening with the load, the government could be asked to come in and help out. The government could give a plot of land and some financial backing where the equipment could be placed. But still, this is a costly solution that cannot happen that often, especially when it comes to bringing together different stakeholders.

To counter the expensive exercise, you can use smartphones to get all the data you need. Today, smartphones have inbuilt three-axis magnetometers. The smartphones are packed with executable programs that help in analyzing magnetometers' readings. In addition to the magnetometers, smartphones also have dozens of sensors including three-axis accelerometers, yaw rate gyros, GPS receivers and temperature sensors, all of which can help undertake the primary measurements.

The two trends of sensor-generated data and mobile computing means that we are going to have more data in the future to come.

2.   The importance of machine learning for the future

Manual labor has lost its footprint in the last 20 years, thanks to the rise of the information age. Job assignments have shifted from the physical attributes of work to the conceptual and more profit based framework. Business has become even hard because of the proliferation of data through the World Wide Web.

This has created a gap of data miners and analyst whose tasks is to help to analyze data for business use. Currently, companies who are developers of software have developed software applications that help business makes sense of big data from any channel of data collection. The ability to synthesize data is going to be a highly sort out skill in the near future. This means that data that is collected from the elementary schools, high schools, colleges and professional institutions have to be understood and presented to make informed decisions.

The data needs to visualized in order for people to understand it even more, and implement it appropriately. Managers need to have access to the data and understand it, it is even more important to have people who have the right skills to communicate analyzed information to managers. Data collection will become more easy to be processed and understood, thanks to machine learning. Below are common terminologies that are found in machine learning that we should mention before going any further.

Key terminology

Before we dive into machine learning algorithms, it is best if we understand terminologies in this field. The best way to go about it is going through a potential system. Our application is a reptile classification system. This is a new field that is interesting to create a machine learning algorithm to make easy to classify reptiles. With the help of computer experts, a computer program will be developed to learn how to identify reptiles. Using all these characteristics, one can decide to measure weight, tail length, whether it has webbed feet, the teeth structure and other factors like poisonous glands. In reality, you would want to measure more details than what we have listed.

With all these attributes changing, how will the application know which reptile is what? This is where the term classification comes into play. To achieve classification, computer machine learning algorithms. It's common practice measure just about anything you can measure and sort out the important parts later.

The four things we've measured are called features; these are also called attributes. For the moment, assume we have all the information from the reptiles. How do we go ahead and decide if a reptile is a frog or something else? This is what is called classification, and presently, there are many machine learning algorithms that work extremely well at classification. We are hereby looking at reptiles and since there are different classification, we can focus on amphibians for this case study.

Once we have the algorithm in place, we need to feed it with training sets for it to learn on how to differentiate reptiles. A nominal value is a variable that is used in regression because its value is continuous. Now, in a training set, its target value is already stated. This is now where the machine learning algorithms become active. When the data is fed, the algorithms will start building relationships between the attributes and the target variable. Now, in our example, the species is our target variable and we can narrow it down further, by taking nominal values.

It is important to note that a training set is a basic measurement that is normally combined with features in the algorithm. To test this machine learning algorithms, there are two different sets of data that are needed, these are, a training set and a test data. The program is first placed with a target variable from the test set of data which helps the program decide the class that the particular program belongs to. At this point, the predicted value is compared to the target value and we then understand the accurate results of the algorithm.

In our classification example, if the results come out as expected, you will be in a great position to say what the machine has learned. This knowledge representation is not normally accurate. This is because some knowledge representation is not comprehensible by us. At times the results are a set of rules or a mathematical equation.

With the algorithm in place, it is time to create a solid application that is working, from a machine language algorithm. It's time to introduce the topic of regression. Regression basically, is how to predict a numerical value. The most common explanation of regression even to an elementary school is, drawing a best-fit line that explains or draws a conclusion to data points.

When we talk about Supervised learning, two important components fall into the category, regression, and classification. Supervised learning can also be defined as when we tell the algorithms what to predict. There is no target value or label for your data classification are instances of supervised learning. When we are telling the algorithm what to predict, this is known as supervised learning.

When we talk about unsupervised learning, we are talking

about the absence of a label or target value for the data.this is where we want to collect the statistical values for data representation- density estimation. This type of learning is tasked to reduce the data to small values that can be observed in dimensions.

How to choose the Right Algorithm

When writing an algorithm, you need to have specifically defined goals. You might be creating a system that predicts the weather tomorrow or a system to select the right games to go for in a betting game. Any solution you are trying to look at needs a lot of data that is specific to it. When you have defined values like this, you will need to be on supervised learning, otherwise, you will have to consider unsupervised learning. In supervised learning, you will need to have a target value. It should be defined, like black or white or Yes and No. You will also have to look into its classification at this point.

If you have numerical target values like let's say -888 to 888, or 1 to 1000, regression is what is advised at this point. Now, when you want to fix some data in groups that you have already structured and defined, then clustering Is what needs to be done. Another way to classify data is through density estimation algorithm, this is when you have numerical data estimates that need to fit in particular groups.

All these rules are not fixed to, but you understand the direction we are looking into. It is imperative to understand the data in order for your application to work as expected. To help you understand what your data should be like, let's take a look some questions that you should ask yourself about the data you are working on:

- Are there any missing values?
- Why is there missing data?
- Are there outliers in the data?
- Is the data nominal or continuous?
- Are you looking for non existence data?

When you answer these questions, you will have a more defined set of data that will help you to build the algorithm more easily.

It is not easy to answer all these questions and come up with the single best appropriate answer to selecting the right algorithm, you will have to test different algorithms and view the results of each algorithm. You can now only imagine the techniques that are used in machine learning. There are even more ways to tweak and improve the performance of machine learning algorithms.

Once the process is done, you will pick the best performing algorithms, maybe two will provide exceptional results and still test more on those. You need to understand that the process of finding the right algorithm needs a repetitive process that is free of errors.

Algorithms have a general basic outline of how they all are built, even though the end results are different. When you come up with the algorithms, you will need all these algorithms in order to achieve a common goal, what we call a functioning application.

Let us look at the guidelines below to approach and build a machine learning application.

1. Collect the data. Use any means possible to get the right data. You can have a collective device to check your blood glucose levels or any other thing you want to measure. The options are endless. To save time, it is possible to use public data that is available.

2. Input data preparation. This is to confirm that your data is of the right format before using it. One common list is the Python list. The benefit of a Python list is that one can mix and match data sources and algorithms.

3. Analyze the data input. Cross check if the data is in full and there are no empty values.

4. In case you are working on a production system, and you have a clue about how the data should look like, you can skip this step if you trust its source. This step is not relevant for an automated system.

5. Training the algorithm. Machine learning takes place at this stage. You feed the algorithm with some clean data from the first two steps, and then you extract information from it. This involves extracting data that has already been parsed in the algorithm. The information is then stored in a usable format that the machine can access easily. In unsupervised learning, there is no training step because no target value exists. The next step uses everything.

6. Testing the algorithm. Test the performance of the algorithm. In supervised learning, there are known values that evaluate an algorithm. You can then use another set of metrics to evaluate the algorithm, this is unsupervised learning. In either case, if you want different results, you can go back to step 4, test again after changing some things. Often the data collection may have been problematic, and you will have to jump to step 1.

7. Using it. Here, you make a program that performs a function.

Probability Theory Classification Using Naive Bayes

In the real application environment, a classifier can make hard decisions. One can ask for some definite answer to the question, for instance, we can ask, "Which class does this instance of data belong to?" There are times when the classifier gets the answer wrong. In these times, we can ask the classifier to give us a different guess about the class and a probability estimate assigned to the best guess.

Many machine-learning algorithms have the probability theory as its basis, so it is important to grasp the topic well. We are going to look at some ways that probability theory can be of service when classifying things. We start with the simple probabilistic classifier, make some assumptions and learn more about the naïve Bayes classifier. It is given the name naïve since it formulates naïve assumptions. This will be clear in a while. We will take full advantage of the text-processing abilities of Python's that helps to split a document to a word vector. This is important to classify text. We will build another classifier use it in the real world and see how it performs in spam email dataset. In case you need a refresher, we will review conditional probability

Classification with Bayesian Decision Theory

An Advantage of Naïve Bayes

- It performs exceptionally well with small bits of data

A disadvantage of Naïve Bayes

- There is a need for attention to the detail when it comes to the data inputs. The best values to work with is the nominal values

What is Bayes?

It is a probability interpretation we use that belongs to a category called Bayesian probability; it works well, and it is popular. Thomas

Bayes, a theologian in the eighteenth-century theologian, was the founder of the Bayesian probability. In Bayesian probability, it is allowed to apply logic and prior knowledge to uncertain statements. Frequency probability is another interpretation which draws conclusions from data, and it does not allow for logic and prior knowledge.

Conditional Probability

Let's take some time and talk about conditional probability and probability.

Let us assume that we have a jar that has 7 balls. Three balls are gray while four balls are black. If we stick a hand into the jar and pull out one ball at random, what are the chances that we pull out a gray ball? There are 7 possible balls, and we have three that are gray. Therefore, the probability is 3/7. What is the probability of grabbing a black ball? It's 4/7. We then write the probability of gray as P(gray). We have calculated the probability of pulling a gray ball P(gray) by counting the gray balls and dividing the figure by the total number of balls.

What if there are seven balls in two jars?

If you want to calculate the P(black) or P(gray), would get to know the bucket change the answer? If you wanted to compute the probability of pulling a gray stone from jar B, you could somehow figure how to do that. This is what is called conditional probability. We are calculating the probability of a gray ball, provided that the unknown ball comes from jar B.

This can be written as:

P(gray | jarB), and this it would read as "the probability of gray given jar B." It is easy to see that P(gray | jarA) is 2/4 and

P(gray | jarB) is 1/3.

To compute the conditional probability, we have

P(gray | jarB) = P(gray and jarB)/P(jarB)

Let's check if there is some sense in this: P(gray and jarB) = 1/7. This was calculated by the number of gray balls in jar B and dividing by the total number of jars. Now,

P(jarB) is 3/7 because there are 3 balls in jar B of the total 7 balls.

Finally, P(gray | jarB) = P(gray and jarB)/P(jarB) = (1/7) / (3/7) = 1/3.

This definition seems like it's too much work for this example, but it will be useful when more features are added. It is also useful to have this definition if we need to manipulate the conditional probability algebraically.

Another important way to manipulate conditional probabilities is called Bayes' rule.

Bayes' rule describes to us how to swap the symbols in a conditional probability statement.

Document classification with Naïve Bayes

Automatic document classification is one important application of machine learning, the whole document which is like an individual email is our instance, and its features are the contents of that email. Email is an instance that keeps popping up, but you can classify message board discussions, news stories, filings with the government, or any text. You can use words to look at the documents and have a feature, the absence or presence of each word. This would give you several features. Naïve Bayes is a well-known algorithm for the document-classification problem.

We are going to use individual words as features and look for the absence or presence of each word. Which (human) Language are we assuming? How many features is that? It may be more than one language. The total number of words in the English language is approximately over 500,000. To read in English, it is said that you need to understand thousands of words. Assuming that our vocabulary is 1,000 words long. To produce good probability distributions, we need some data samples. Let us use N as the number of samples. Statistics show us that if for one feature, we need N samples, then for 10 features we need N10 and for our 1,000-feature Vocabulary, we need N1000. The number gets large very quickly.

If we assume statistical independence, then our N1000

data points are reduced to 1000*N. One word or feature is just as likely by itself as it is next to other words. If we assume that the word bacon is going to appear next to the word unhealthy because it is next to delicious, this assumption is not true; because we know that bacon almost always appears close to delicious but not close to unhealthy. This is what is meant by naïve in the naïve Bayes classifier.

One assumption we make is that every feature is important which is not true. If we were to classify a message board posting as inappropriate, we only need to look at maybe 10 or 20 and not to look at 1,000 words. Despite the assumptions' flaws, naïve Bayes does well practically. At this point, you can get into some code with the basics you have acquired about this topic.

How to approach to naïve Bayes

1. Data collection: We can use RSS feeds as an example.

2. Preparation: Boolean or Numeric values.

3. Analyze: Looking at histograms is a better idea when looking at many features

4. Training: You will have to perform calculations of the independent attributes to find the conditional probabilities of independent features.

5. Test: Calculate the error rate.

6. Implementation: Naïve Bayes can be used in any classification setting, not necessarily in a text.

4.5 Classifying Text With Python

To get features from our text, the text needs to be split up. But how to do that is the question. Our features are going to be tokens from the text. A token is any character combination. Think of tokens as words, but we may also use other characters which are not words including IP addresses, URLs or any other set of characters. We'll reduce every text to a vector of tokens where the token existing in the document is represented by 1 and 0 represents its absence.

Let's make a quick filter to see this in action. This filter is on an online message board that flags an inappropriate message if the author uses abusive or negative language. This kind of filtering is common because negative postings can damage an online community;'s online reputation. We are going to have two categories: abusive and not abusive. We'll use 1 to represent abusive and 0 to represent not abusive.

- First, we're going to create a vector of numbers from transform lists of text.
- Next, from these vectors, we will show how to compute conditional probabilities.
- Then, we will create a classifier and then look at practical considerations on how to implement naïve Bayes in Python.

Preparation: Making Word Vectors from Text

We are now going to look at the text in terms of token vectors or word vectors, and see how we can transform a sentence to become a vector. All the words in our documents will be considered and then we will decide what we will use for a set of words or vocabulary that we will consider. Next, we will transform each document to a vector from a vocabulary.

Now we can look at the functions being actualised. Save bayes.py, and input the following into your Python shell:

```
>>> import bayes

>>> listOPosts,listClasses = bayes.loadDataSet()

>>> myVocabList = bayes.create
VocabuList(listOPosts)

>>> myVocabList
```

['cute', 'love', 'help', 'garbage', 'quit', 'I', 'problems', 'is', 'park',

'stop', 'flea', 'hound', 'licks', 'food', 'not', 'him', 'buying',

'posting', 'has', 'worthless', 'ate', 'to', 'maybe', 'please', 'dog',

'how', 'stupid', 'so', 'take', 'mr', 'steak', 'my']

After examining this list, you will see no repeated words. The list is

unsorted, and if you want to sort it, you can do that later.

Let's look at the next function setOfWords2Vec():

```
>>> bayes.setOfWords2Vec(myVocabList,
listOPosts[0])
```

[0, 0, 1, 0, 0, 0, 1, 0, 0, 0, 1, 0, 0, 0, 0, 0, 0, 0, 1, 0, 0, 0, 0, 1, 1,

0, 0, 0, 0, 0, 0, 1]

>>> bayes.setOfWords2Vec(myVocabList, listOPosts[3])

[0, 0, 0, 1, 0, 0, 0, 0, 0, 1, 0, 0, 0, 0, 0, 0, 0, 1, 0, 1, 0, 0, 0, 0, 0,

0, 1, 0, 0, 0, 0, 0]

Create a vector

D of all 0s

This has taken our vocabulary list that you would like to examine and create a feature for each of them. Now when you apply a given document (a posting to

the hound site), it will be transformed to a word vector. Check to see if this makes sense. What's the word at index 2 in myVocabList? It should help. This word should be in our first document. Now check to see that it isn't in our fourth document.

Logistic Regression

If you think about it, we always look at ways we can optimize problems in our daily lives. Some optimizations from daily life are these:

- How do we travel from point A to point B in the shortest time possible?

- How do we make huge returns or profits while doing the least amount of work?
- How do we design a high-performance engine that produces the most horsepower using the least amount of fuel?

Optimization has made it possible for us to do powerful things. We are going to look at several optimization algorithms to train a nonlinear function for classification.

If regression is not familiar to you, it's fine. You might have seen some data points on a graph, and then someone places the best-fit line to these points; this is what we call regression. In logistic regression, there is a bunch of data, and an equation is built to perform a classification with the data. The regression aspects mean that we look at finding a best-fit set of parameters. Finding the best fit is just like regression, and that is how we train our classifier. We'll use optimization algorithms to find these best-fit parameters.

How To Approach Logistic Regression

1. Data collection: any method can be used

2. Preparation: for a distance calculation, use Numeric values. It is best to use a structured data format.

3. Analyze: use any method.

4. Training: most of the time will be spent training, where optimal coefficients to classify our data will be looked at.

5. Testing: Classification is fast and easy once the training step is over.

6. Using: This application needs some input data, and an

output structured numeric values.Then, the application applies simple regression calculation on

the input data and determines the destined input data class it belongs to. Some action on the calculated class is taken by the application.

Preparation: Dealing With Missing Values in the Data

If you have data and there are missing values, it is a big problem, and there are textbooks dedicated to solving this issue. Well, why is it a problem? Let's take an example where we have 100 instances with 20 features, and a machine collected the data. What if a machine's sensor was broken and a feature was useless? is all the data disposable? What of the 19 other features that are remaining; are they any more relevant? Yes, they do. Data is expensive sometimes, and throwing it all out is not an option, so you a method has to be identified to handle the problem.

Here are some options:

■ Use the mean value of the feature from the available data.

■ A special value like -1 is used to fill in the unknown.

■ Ignore the instance.

■ Similar items use the same mean value.

■ To predict the value, use another machine learning algorithm.

During the preprocessing, you can decide to do two things

from the list. You can first replace all unknown values with a real number since we are using NumPy, and in NumPy arrays can't miss a value. The number 0 was chosen, which works well for logistic regression. The reasoning is: we want a value that will not impact the weight when updating. The weights are updated depending on

weights = weights + alpha * error * dataMatrix[randIndex]

If any feature's DataMatrix is 0, then the feature's weight will simply be weights = weights

Also, this won't impact the error term because of sigmoid(0)=0.5, is neutral for class prediction. This, therefore, indicates that placing o in places where there are missing values allows us to avoid compromising the learning algorithm while keeping our imperfect data. In some sense, no features take 0 in the data; it is just a special value. Second, the test data was missing a class label. It's difficult to replace a missing class label. This solution is important when using logistic regression, but it is likely not to make sense with kNN.

From its original form, the data was preprocessed and modified in two files. Since we have a good optimization algorithm and a clean set of data, we will put all these pieces together and build a classifier to try and see if we can predict whether colic will be the cause of death of a horse.

Test: Classifying with Logistic Regression

With logistic regression not much needs to be done when

classifying an instance. All one needs to calculate is the sigmoid of the vector being tested multiplied by the earlier optimized weights. If the sigmoid produces a value greater than 0.5, the class is 1, and 0 if otherwise.

If the value of the sigmoid is more than 0.5, it's considered a 1; otherwise, it's a 0. The colicTest() is normally a standalone function that opens the training set, test set and properly formats the data. First, the loading of the training set is done, where the last column contains the class value. At first, the data can contain three class values representing what happened to the horse: lived, euthanized or died. For this exercise, you can then combine euthanized and died into a category called "did not live." After loading this data, we will use stocGradAscent1() to calculate the weights vector. After using 500 iterations to train the weights; it improves performance over the default 150 iterations. You can change this value as expected. After calculating the weights, you can load the test set and calculate an error rate. ColicTest() is totally a standalone function. If it is run multiple times with its random components, you will have different results. If the weights converged in stocGradAscent1(), then no random components would be available.

The last function takes after using the average, multiTest(), and running the function colicTest() 10 times. After running test script with some input data, the analysis might look like this.

The data had a 35% error rate after 10 iterations. This was not bad having 30% of the values missing. To get results approaching a 20% error rate, you can alter the alpha size in stochGradAscent1() and also the number of iterations in colicTest().

Summary

- Logistic regression means finding the best-fit parameters to a nonlinear function that is termed as the sigmoid.
- One of the most common optimization algorithms is the gradient ascent.
- Finding the best-fit parameters requires methods of optimization.
- Stochastic gradient ascent simplifies the Gradient.
- Stochastic gradient ascent uses fewer computing resources compared to gradient ascent. Stochastic gradient ascent is an online algorithm that does not load data like batch processing, instead, it can update what it has learned while new data comes in.
- How to deal with missing values in the data is a major problem in machine learning. There is no overall answer to this question. It depends on your intention with the data. There are some solutions, and each solution has its pros and cons.

Upgrading Classification Using AdaBoost Meta-Algorithm

If you happen to be in a defining position where you have to decide on the future of a business, it is obvious for one to rely on several opinions that just one. Why should we have it any other way when it comes to machine learning? The way this is done in machine learning is by the use of meta-algorithms. These involve the combination of different algorithms. We are going to look at AdaBoost to understand what we mean by this.AdaBoost is considered to the best-supervised learning algorithm; it is a MUST have tool that should be in your toolbox.

Classifiers Using Multiple Samples of the Dataset

There are different algorithms for classification which when you perform a SWOT analysis, you will see how important it is to combine multiple classifiers. Meta-algorithms or ensemble methods come into play in this instance. Ensemble methods take the same algorithm having different settings, then they use different algorithms, or they are assigned different dataset parts to different classifiers.

Bagging: A Way to Build Classifiers from Random Data

Bagging which is also identified as Bootstrap aggregating is a way that involves an original data sets component makes a totally new dataset. The two are normally of the same size.

You will need random examples from the original dataset "with replacement," this means that the same dataset can be used repetitively. "with replacement" allows repeated values in a dataset and the new set will miss the original values. A learning algorithm is applied to each dataset after building the S datasets. When classifying a new data piece, you can take a majority vote by applying the S classifier.

AdaBoost

- Pros: easy to code, Low generalization error, no parameters to adjust and it works with most classifiers,

- Cons: It is sensitive to outliers. Works well with both nominal and Numeric values

There are more advanced bagging methods like random forests. Let us turn our attention to boosting, which works almost the same way as the bagging method.

Boosting

Boosting and bagging are comparatively similar techniques. When you get into both techniques, you will find that the same classifier is used. When you get to boosting, you will realize that the different classifiers that are being used are trained on a sequential basis. Each new classifier is trained in the same manner that the previous classifiers were trained on. When boosting is done, classifiers are led to concentrate on misclassified data that was done by previous classifiers.

The difference between boosting and bagging comes in on output calculations. In boosting, the output calculation comes from the weighted sum of the classifiers that are in it. When you compare the weights on bagging and boosting, you will see the difference. In bagging, you have to know that the out is dependent on the success of a classifier was in the previous sections. There are very many boosting version, but we will focus on AdaBoost, which is the most popular version.

How to approach AdaBoost

1. Collection: Find the best way to collect the data.

2. Preparation: Choose a weak learner, use decision stumps and use a simple classifier in this process.

3. Analyze: There are different ways you can check the quality of the data.

4. Training: train the weak learners over and over on the same dataset.

5. Testing: Test the dataset over and over and check the error rates.

6. Use: AdaBoost predicts one of two classes just like support vector machines.

If you want to use it for classification involving more than two classes, you will have to apply some of the same methods as for support vector machines.

AdaBoost and support vector machines are the most powerful algorithms in supervised learning. The two are similar in a couple of ways. First, the kernel of the support vector machines is the weak learner in AdaBoost. The AdaBoost algorithm can be written regarding maximizing a minimum margin. Margins are calculated in different ways which lead to different results majorly when it comes to higher dimensions.

Classification Imbalance

Imagine someone brings a horse, asks us to make a prediction on whether the horse will die or not. If dying is our decision and we are delaying the obvious outcome, then the last option is to have the horse euthanized. After all, if we predict wrong, the horse would have lived. If we predicted incorrectly our where our classifier is only 80% accurate, we would have subjected the horse to a death penalty.

Let's dive into spam detection. It is not even conceivable to allow spam emails to get to the inbox. There are many examples of this nature, and we can say that the cost is never equal.

Sampling of Data and Working Around Classification Imbalance

Classifiers are tuned to change the data that trains classifiers that deal with imbalanced tasks if classification. This is achieved by data undersampling and oversampling.

When we talk about undersampling, it means to sample deleting while oversample means to duplicate samples. Whichever way you choose, you will be altering data. Sampling is done either randomly or through a specific structured process. Normally, there is a rare case of credit card fraud that you're trying to identify. You want to preserve enough information about the rare case, so you should store all positive and undersample examples, and the discard negative examples from the negative class.

One disadvantage is choosing one negative disadvantage to do away with. When you make the decision on which example to remove, you might toss out valuable information that is not contained the other examples.

A solution for this is picking samples to toss that is not close to the decision boundary. We can take an example and say that you have a dataset with 50 credit card transactions that are fraudulent and you also have transactions which are legitimate counting to 5,000. To equally balance the set of data then about 4950 of the legitimate transactions will have to be disregarded and removed. Although these examples may contain critical information and this seems severe, therefore, it is prudent that a cross mix approach is used so that out of the two sets of samples, oversampling the positive set and undersampling of the negative set is considered as the other alternative that can be used.

For the oversample of the positive set, put in new points that are identical to those points already existing or replicate the existing examples. One method to consider is to add one data point interpolated in between the already existing data point. This results to overfitting.

Summary

- Instead of simply using one classifier, ensemble methods far better ways since they combine the possible outcomes of the multiple classifiers in order to arrive at a more suitable and fitting answer. We have decided to regard at the techniques using only one type of classifier even though there are combinations of techniques that use various types of classifiers. In mixing multiple classifiers this seeks to make the most of the shortcomings of single classifiers, like overfitting. Since the classifiers are different from each other, combining multiple classifiers can help. This difference can be in the use of data to that algorithm or used to make up the algorithm. The two types of techniques ensembles we discussing are are boosting and bagging. Boosting involves borrowing and taking the idea of bagging more further by the application of a different classifier consecutively to a dataset.

- When it comes to bagging, datasets that are of similar size as the original dataset are made up by sampling examples in a random manner for the dataset with replacement. Random forests are an extra ensemble technique successfully used. Random forests are not as popular as AdaBoost. AdaBoost uses the base classifier as a weak learner, with the weight vector weighing the input data.

Data is equally weighted in the first iteration. If data was incorrectly classified previously, then in the consecutive iterations the data is weighted more strongly. This is the strength that's associated with AdaBoost, its adaptive nature of the errors previously done. By using AdaBoost, then the functions that are built to create the classifier and decision stumps which are the weak learner. When the weighted data is well appropriated by the classifier, then the functions of the AdaBoost can be applied to any classifier. The AdaBoost algorithm shows how powerful it is by quickly handling datasets that other classifiers found to be difficult. The imbalance problem of classification is training a classifier with data which the negative and positive examples are not equal. The negative and positive examples have different misclassification costs, a problem normally arises.

CHAPTER 2
USING REGRESSION TO FORECAST
NUMERIC VALUES

Tree-based Regression

One way to model our data is to subdivide it into sections that we can use to build a model with ease. Using linear regression techniques, these partitions can then be modeled. If we first partition the data and the results don't fit a linear model, then we can partition the partitions. Recursion and Trees are useful tools when it comes to partitioning. We will first look at CART, a new algorithm for building trees. CART stands for Classification And Regression Trees. It can be applied to classification or regression, so it is a valuable tool to learn.

Using CART for Regression

To model complex data interactions, we have decided to use trees to partition the data. How will partitions be split up? How will we know when we have split up the data enough? It all depends on how we're modeling the final values. The regression tree method uses a tree to break up data with constant values on the leaf nodes. This strategy assumes that we can summarize the complex interactions of the data.

To construct a tree of piecewise constant values, we need to measure the consistency of data. How can we gauge the disorder of continuous values? It is quite easy to measure a disorder for a set of data. We will have to calculate first the mean value of a set and find the data deviation of each piece of this mean value. To treat both positive and negative deviations equally, we have to get the magnitude of the deviation from the mean. The magnitude can be gotten with the squared value or the absolute value. Calculating the variance is very common in statistics. The only difference is that the variance is the mean squared error and we are looking for the total error. We can get this total squared error by multiplying the variance of a dataset by the number of elements in a dataset.

With a tree-building algorithm and this error rule, it is possible to write code to construct a regression tree from a dataset.

Tree Pruning

An example of a model overfit is a tree with too many nodes. Pruning is the procedure of reducing the complexity of a decision tree to avoid overfitting.

Post Pruning

In this method, to begin with, you will have to separate the data into a training set and a test set. First, you will build a tree with the setting that will give you the largest, most complex tree. You will then descend the tree until you reach a node that has only leaves. You will use a test set to test the leaves against data and measure if merging the leaves are going to give you less error on the test set. If merging the nodes will reduce the error on the test set, you will merge the nodes.

Pseudo-code for prune() representation:

In a given tree, split the test data:

If the either split is a tree: call prune on that split

Compute the error after merging two leaf nodes

Without merging, compute the error

Merge the leaf nodes if merging results is in lower error

One way to model our data is to subdivide it into sections that we can use to build a model with ease. Using linear regression techniques, these partitions can then be modeled. If we first partition the data and the results don't fit a linear model, then we can partition the partitions. Recursion and Trees are useful tools when it comes to partitioning. We will first look at CART, a new algorithm for building trees. CART stands for Classification And Regression Trees. It can be applied to classification or regression, so it is a valuable tool to learn.

Often, your data has complex interactions that lead to nonlinear relationships between the input data and the target variables. To model these complex relationships, one can use a tree to break up the predicted value into piecewise linear segments or piecewise constant segments.

A regression tree is a tree structure that models the data with piecewise constant segments. If the models are linear regression equations, the tree is called a model tree.

The CART algorithm builds binary trees handles continuous split values as well as discrete values. Model trees and regression trees can be built with the CART algorithm as long as the right error measurements are used. There is a tendency for the tree-building algorithm to build the tree too close to the data when building a tree; this results in an overfit model. There is normally a lot of complexity when it comes to an overfit tree. A process of pruning is applied to the tree to make it less complex. Two methods of pruning are normally available, pre-pruning, which prunes the tree as in the building phase, and post-pruning, which prunes the tree after the building phase is complete. Pre-pruning is more effective, but it requires user-defined parameters.

Tkinter is the most commonly used GUI toolkit for Python. Tkinter allows one to build widgets and arrange them. You can create a special widget for Tkinter that allows you to display Matplotlib plots. The integration of Matplotlib and Tkinter allows you to build powerful GUIs where people can explore machine learning algorithms more naturally.

CHAPTER 3
UNSUPERVISED LEARNING

Grouping Items that Are Not Labeled Using K-means Clustering

When running a presidential election, it is possible to have the winner come out victories with a very small margin from the 1st runner up. An example is when the popular vote that a candidate receives is 50.7%, and the lowest is 47.9%. If a particular percentage of the voters are to cross to the other side, then the outcome of the election can be different. In an election period, there is group of voters who can be compelled to switch sides. These groups may be small, but with close races like the one we are describing, the groups may turn out to be big enough to alter the election's outcome

Now, how does one find these "small" groups of people, and how does one appeal to them with a small budget? The answer to this question is clustering. Let us look at how it is done. First, you will need to collect people's information with or without their approval: any information that might give a clue on what triggers can influence them. Then input the results into a clustering algorithm. Afterward, choose the largest first for each cluster and prepare a message that will appeal to them. Finally, you will start your campaign and track its performance.

Clustering is automatically forming groups of things that are similar; it is a type of unsupervised learning, and it is also like an automatic classification. You can cluster anything, clusters are always better if there are more similar items in one cluster; the more similar the items are in the cluster, the better your clusters are. We are going to study one type of clustering algorithm called k-means. It's called K means because it finds k unique clusters, and the center of each cluster is the mean of the values in that cluster. You'll see this in more detail in a little bit.

Before we get into k-means, let's talk about cluster identification. Cluster identification tells an algorithm, "Here's some data. Now group similar things together and tell me about those groups." The key difference from classification is that in classification you know what you're looking for. That's not the case in clustering. Clustering is sometimes called unsupervised classification because it produces the same result as classification but without having predefined classes.

With cluster analysis, we're trying to put similar things in a cluster and dissimilar things in a different cluster. This notion of similarity depends on a similarity measurement.

You've seen different similarity measures in previous chapters, and they'll come up in later chapters as well. The type of similarity measure used depends on the application. We'll build the k-means algorithm and see it in action. We'll next discuss some simple k-means algorithm drawbacks. To work on some of these problems, we can apply post processing to produce better clusters. Next, you'll see a more efficient version of k-means called bisecting k-means. Finally, you'll see an example where we'll use bisecting k-means to find optimal parking locations while visiting multiple nightlife hotspots.

The k-means clustering algorithm

- Advantage:
  Implementation is easy

- Disadvantage:
  It is slow on large datasets

  The algorithm accommodates numeric values

  It can converge at local minima

In the k-means algorithm, k clusters will be found first for a particular dataset. The k clusters that will be found will be user defined. A single point which is known as the centroid describes each cluster. The term Centroid means that it's located the center of all the points in the cluster. This is how the k-means algorithm works. First, the k centroids are randomly assigned to a point. Next, each point in the dataset is assigned to a cluster. The assignment is done by finding the closest centroid and assigning the point to that cluster. After this step, the centroids are all updated by taking the mean value of all the points in that cluster.

Here's how the pseudo-code would look:

Create k points randomly for starting centroids

While any point has changed the cluster cluster

for every dataset point:

for every centroid

compute the distance between the point and the centroid

the cluster is assigned to the point with the lowest distance

for every cluster compute the mean of the points in that cluster

the mean is assigned the centroid

General approach to k-means clustering

1. Collecting: use of different data collection methods is okay

2. Preparing: Nominal values and distance computing require nominal values

3. Analyze: Use any data analysis method.

4. Training: it is only available in supervised learning

5. Testing: Check the output of the clustering algorithm during testing. You can use Quantitative error

Measurements like the of squared error.

6. Use: Anything available works.

Bisecting k-means

An algorithm that is known as bisecting -means has been developed to counter the poor clusters problem. It starts out with one cluster and then splits the cluster in two. It then chooses a cluster to split. The cluster to split is decided by minimizing the SSE. This splitting based on the SSE is repeated until the user-defined number of clusters is obtained.

Pseudocode for bisecting k-means will look like this:

Begin with all the points in a cluster

While cluster numbers is less than k

for each cluster

measure the total error

k-means is then performed with k=2 on the given cluster

The total error is measured after k-means has split the cluster in two

choose the cluster split that gives the lowest error and commit this split

Another way of thinking about this is to choose the cluster with the largest SSE and split it and then repeat until you get to the user-defined number of clusters. This doesn't sound too difficult to code, does it? To see this in action, open kMeans.py and enter the code from the following listing.

Example: clustering points on a map

> Here's the situation: your friend Drew wants you to
> take him out on the town for his birthday. Some
> other friends are going to come also, so you need to
> provide a plan that everyone can follow. Drew has
> given you a list of places he wants to go. This list is
> long; it has 70 establishments in it. I included the list
> in a file called portland-Clubs.txt, which is packaged
> with the code. The list contains similar establishments
> in the greater Portland, Oregon, area.
>
> Seventy places in one night! You decide the best
> strategy is to cluster these places together. You can
> arrange transportation to the cluster centers and then
> hit the places on foot. Drew's list includes addresses,
> but addresses don't give you a lot of information
> about how close two places are. What you need are
> the latitude and longitude. Then, you can cluster these
> places together and plan your trip.

Example: using bisecting k-means on geographic data

1. Collect: Use the Yahoo! PlaceFinder API to collect data.

2. Preparation: Remove all data except latitude and longitude.

3.Analyze: Use Matplotlib to make 2D plots of our data, with clusters and map.

4.Train: It is only available in supervised learning.

5. Test: Use biKmeans().

6.Use: The final product will be your map with the clusters and cluster centers.

You need a service that will convert an address to latitude and longitude. Luckily, Yahoo! provides such a service. Where you will explore how to use the Yahoo! PlaceFinder API. Then, we'll cluster our coordinates and plot the coordinates along with cluster centers to see how good our clustering job was.

The Yahoo! PlaceFinder API. The wonderful people at Yahoo! have provided a free API that will return a latitude and longitude for a given address. You can read more about it at the following URL:

http://developer.yahoo.com/geo/placefinder/guide/.

1. In order to use it, you need to sign up for an API key. To do that, you have to sign up for the Yahoo! Developer Network: http://developer.yahoo.com/.

CHAPTER 4
WHERE TO GO FROM HERE

Career Opportunities

These are some of the skills one needs to have to take advantage of the ever growing career opportunities in Machine learning.

1. Fundamentals of Computer Science and Programming

Machine learning is dependent on basics that are studied in computer science. Some of these basics include: (sorting, searching, dynamic programming, optimization e.t.c), data structures (queues, trees, multi-dimensional arrays, stacks, graphs e.t.c), computability and complexity (approximate algorithms, big-O notation, NP-complete problems, P vs. NP etc.), and computer architecture (distributed processing, bandwidth, deadlocks, cache, memory e.t.c)

You have to be ready to implement, address and adapt to these fundamentals. When you are programming. To improve and hone your skills, you need to engage in hackathons, coding competitions, and practice problems.

2. Probability and Statistics

Probability characteristics (Bayes rule, independence, conditional probability, likelihood, e.t.c) and techniques that are derived from (Hidden Markov, Markov Decision Processes, Bayes Nets, e.t.c.) the basis of Machine Learning algorithms.

These are the ways that help in dealing with real world problems that are elusive to us.

To gather a relationship with this field, the most relatable field is the field of statistics which has in its provision important measures like the median, mean and standard deviation. Distributions that include binomial, Poisson, normal and uniform are usable. To add, analysis methods like hypothesis testing and ANOVA are also available method necessary for model building and validation from data that is observed. For this basis, it is evident that machine learning is an extension of procedures that are in statistical modeling.

3. Evaluation and Data Modeling

When you describe data modeling, what should come to mind is that it is an estimation process that occurs on the datasets underlying structure, targeting discovering patterns that are useful. They include eigenvectors, clusters, correlation e.t.c. anticipating and speculating properties of unseen instances like regression, anomaly detection, classification e.t.c. An important part of this process is the continuous evaluation of how a model is. You will have to choose an accuracy measure depending on the task you are working on, for instance, sum-of-squared-errors for regression, log-loss for classification, e.t.c) and a strategy evaluation like sequential vs randomized cross-validation or training-testing split, e.t.c. Learning algorithms that are iterative directly use emanating errors to changing the model like backpropagation on neural networks. Therefore, understanding the measures is important for even applying standard algorithms.

4. Machine Learning Algorithms and Libraries Application

Machine Learning algorithms standard applications are available through APIs (e.g. Tensor Flow, Theano, scikit-learn, Spark MLlib, H2O etc.), packages, libraries. Using them involves picking a suitable structure, a procedure of learning to fit the data (gradient descent, linear regression, bagging, boosting, algorithms to do with genetics and other model-specific techniques and getting a grip of how learning is affected by parameters. You should also be acquitted the disadvantages and advantages of various approaches and gotchas that can trip one (overfitting and underfitting, bias and variance, data leakage, missing data etc) Machine Learning challenge and Data Science are exciting ways to discover new problems and their respective nuances.

5. System Design and Software Engineering

For any Machine Learning Engineer, the typical output is a

software. This is a part of a larger integrated system of

products and services. One needs to get how different pieces relate (using REST APIs, library calls, database queries, e.t.c) and work together and build interfaces for these components that will make others depend on. It is necessary to design careful system designs to circumvent problems and with the increasing big data then your algorithms scale with it.

Some of the best practices in software engineering include requirements analysis, modularity, designing of the system, testing, documentation, version control, e.t.c are available for collaboration, productivity, maintainability, and quality.

CHAPTER 5
THE FUTURE OF EMPLOYMENT

How Jobs are Susceptible to Computerization

We are going to look at the potential future risks that job computerization will bring to the table and the related labor market outcomes. It has been predicted that new developments in ML will help to bring down the accumulated demand for labor input in tasks that can be routinized via recognition of patterns while increasing the labor demand for those tasks that are not vulnerable to computerization.

It's not possible to predict the future changes in the labor market, and we don't intend to do that. This is because, according to a BLS occupational employment projections that were conducted in 2010, it is tough to predict US net employment growth in different business fields based on the historical patterns. Technology is starting to proliferate into different sectors, and we cannot speculate how far technology will impact the business environment. This means that the data we have on the technological impact is still growing and we need to continuously observe it.

We are at this moment limited to how future computerization will be subject to substitution. In the next few decades, developments in computerization will tend to rely on the progress of the issues described above will be overcome. Looking at it in this kind of perspective, the results are comparable in two sets of computations that are split by a "technological plateau."

Workers in logistics and transportation occupations, together with the administrative support and bulk of office, will characterize by the first wave together; and computer capital will be on the way of replacing production occupations. We are seeing a rise in computerized cars which has led to the decrease of the high price of sensors, that makes creating vehicles that have been upgraded with advanced sensors, increasingly economical. The automation of logistics occupations and transportation is going to increase rapidly with the tech advancements coming on board to make it easier to send items across the world. We are now seeing how big data algorithms are getting into the domains that store information, making it possible for office operations to be subject to computerization.

As there is an increase in industrial robots which are advancing in capability and efficiency, they are tasked with operating non-manual tasks across the board. In the next few decades, we are also going to see a cut down on production occupations, as this field is going to be a less common employment field. If you look at the landscape when it comes to service, construction, and even sales occupations, we will also expect to see computerization of these tasks.

Limitations

Our future projections are based on forecasting on the fact that we are going to see computerizations in the new future materializing. Therefore, we are focusing on making an estimate of the employment field that can be replaced by artificial intelligence.

We will not make any attempt to measure the jobs that will be replaced by computers. There are several factors that will lead to the actual pace and extent of computerization.

First, if human capital costs are relatively high or the access to cheap labor is scarce, innovations of making labor cheap may be considered. For example, it has been documented that production of cotton in Britain in the eighteenth century, relative to other countries, Britain's wage levels were very higher. Also, recent empirical research does not account for capital prices, labor shortages or future wage levels. As these factors have the capacity to impact the timeline of our predictions, the scarce factor is labor. This means that employment will be increasing directly proportional to capital prices, and this will make all automated operations profitable.

Second, political activism and regulatory concerns may slow down the computerization process. The states of Nevada and California have made a legislative change to allow for driverless cars. Other states are also following suit. The pace and extent of legislation are dependent also on the advancement of technology that the public is accepting. Although since the Industrial Revolution, there has been a slowing resistance to technological change. We are avoiding to declare that technological progress, predictive legislative process and the pace of computerization is evident to all.

Third, it is difficult to make predictions about technological progression. This leads us to focus on the innovations that we are making in technology, in Machine Learning, to avoid making projections that have a task to overcome several engineering bottlenecks in computerization. Finally, we are not going to look into the slight changes that computerization makes in some small tasks that facilitate the growth of human labor.

For examples, the former Britain politician William Huskisson was killed during the opening ceremony of a railway locomotive that was being launched in Liverpool and Manchester Railway. This incident dissuaded the public from technology in railway transportation. By contrast, technology in an airship is widely recognized and it lost the attention of many veterans in the industry because of the outcome of the Hindenburg disaster.

Uber, one of the fasted mobile app company that has ever existed, connects drivers to passengers, has been criticized by regulators from different countries because of the price wars that the taxi service has been experiencing. Marvin Minsky in 1970, famously claimed that "in the next decade we will have a machine with the general intelligence of an average human being." This estimation is yet to materialize.

Our findings have shown that with the advancement in technology, we are going to see the workers who don't have sufficient skills, will be tasked to do jobs that computers cannot automate. These tasks require social and creative intelligence. To be at the top of their game, workers will have to learn and become knowledgeable in skills that are both creative and social.

CONCLUSION

Thanks for making it through to the end of Machine Learning, we hope that is was informative enough, and you have been provided with the tools necessary to either improve your skills or help you prepare more on Machine Learning and computerizations. Finishing this book is just the beginning since you will open up into the world of programming in Python and other languages. The future is software, and we hope you will carry on with learning more.

We hope you will learn one or two programming languages to prepare for the change that businesses will be gearing to. There are careers that are becoming obsolete due to computerization, and it is a high time that we embrace technology, learn and evolve with the new career opportunities that will be available.

Recently, we have seen how technology has changed different fields, from finance to medicine and other fields. There are fields that might not be affected that much with computerization, but when interacting with other fields, everyone is liable to change in some way. The opportunities that are coming are great, and they will help us solve some of the world's solutions. It is only best if we prepare our children and ourselves to learn about the new world that will be powered by technology early enough. Look for the opportunities that you can evolve within your field of work and model your future with it.

Finally, if you found this book useful in any way, a review on Amazon is always appreciated!